D0426640

CONTENTS:

Acknowledgments

A. A. Pare of Miami, Florida and Garrie Landry of Franklin, Louisiana helped me obtain some of the birds I needed. J. A. W. Prior of the Zebra Finch Society, London, England graciously permitted the Standards and Show Cage Specifications of the Society to be included in this book.

My wife Edith May patiently typed the manuscript and ferreted out a tremendous number of spelling errors; I hope she caught the worst of them.

Mervin F. Roberts
Old Lyme, Connecticut

Photo Credits
M.F. Roberts: 51 (bottom), 64, 66, 70; W. Starika: 23, 79; Heinz Schrempp: 15; Glen S. Axelrod: 47, 51 (top); Harry V. Lacey: front and back endpapers, frontis, 6 (bottom), 7, 8, 9, 14 (bottom), 20, 21, 22 (top), 26 (bottom), 28, 29, 32, 33, 37, 42, 43, 44, 62, 65, 67, 75, 80, 81, 85. Courtesy of Vogelpark Walsrode: 6 (top), 10, 11, 14 (top), 18, 19, 26 (top), 30, 31, 71, 82, 83, 86, 87, 90, 91; K. Scott Kilner: 17; J. Wessels; 22 (bottom); Paul Kwast: 27.

Drawings:
R.A. Vowles: 74 (bottom); Heinzel: 74 (top), 78.

ISBN 0-87666-882-1

© 1981 by T.F.H. Publications, Inc. Ltd.

Distributed in the U.S. by T.F.H. Publications, Inc., 211 West Sylvania Avenue, PO Box 427, Neptune, NJ 07753; in England by T.F.H. (Gt. Britain) Ltd., 13 Nutley Lane, Reigate, Surrey; in Canada to the pet trade by Rolf C. Hagen Ltd., 3225 Sartelon Street, Montreal 382, Quebec; in Canada to the book trade by H & L Pet Supplies, Inc., 27 Kingston Crescent, Kitchener, Ontario N28 2T6; in Southeast Asia by Y.W. Ong, 9 Lorong 36 Geylang, Singapore 14; in Australia and the South Pacific by Pet Imports Pty. Ltd., P.O. Box 149, Brookvale 2100, N.S.W. Australia; in South Africa by Valid Agencies, P.O. Box 51901, Randburg 2125 South Africa. Published by T.F.H. Publications, Inc., Ltd., the British Crown Colony of Hong Kong.

ZEBRA FINCHES

MERVIN F. ROBERTS

Through selective breeding and application of genetic principles, pied (1), fawn (2), white (3, middle bird) and many other color and pattern varieties have been developed—but they are all one-hundred percent zebra finch.

2

Left: That this zebra finch is a male is evidenced by the cheek marks, the striping across the throat and breast and the flanks with white spots. **Below:** The adult male on the left is accompanied by three juveniles, told by their blackish bills. The striping coming in on the throat and breast of the youngster in the center shows what his sex will be.

Introduction

People who have studied the pet industry will generally agree that, nine out of ten times, the initial purchase in a pet shop is an impulsive purchase of a living thing. Hardly anyone (at least in the U. S. A.) first buys a book to research the subject, then purchases the empty aquarium and finally gets the fish. Same goes for birds. You chose a zebra finch or two. Then you bought a cage or resolved to use that old canary cage sitting forgotten on a shelf for lo these many years. Then you bought this book. Well, that's still all right. Even without the book, you made a wise decision when you chose zebra finches. They are hardy, inexpensive to maintain, long-lived, active and attractive. With your permission (and little else) they will breed even in a relatively small cage. They are quiet at night; they don't smell. They come in several color patterns, they get along well with each other and with many other cage birds also.

(1,2) Side and front views of a gray male zebra. (3,4) Back and front views of a fawn male. **Inset:** A yellow-billed fawn female.

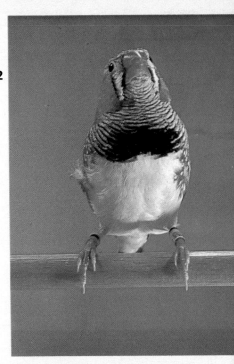

(1,2) Two views of a gray female. **Inset:** A yellow-billed gray female.
(3,4) Two views of a fawn female.

They are good for beginners but are nevertheless favorites of many advanced aviculturists. They tolerate wide fluctuations in temperature; if their bath water freezes, you have but to break the ice and they will be in and splashing. They thrive on inexpensive millet supplemented by items from your kitchen. You should have started with zebra finches long ago!

There is no need to describe here the feathering, colors and markings on zebra finches. The pictures and the Zebra Finch Society Standards do a better job, so let's just look at the branch of the tree of life where the little bird sits, because I believe this is a good way to begin a proper introduction.

Animalia—the animal kingdom, which includes all living things except plants and fungi.

Chordata—the phylum with dorsal nervous systems.

Vertebrata—the subphylum with bones or cartilage around these dorsally located nerves. Some older books call it a phylum.

Craniata—with a skull at one end of the vertebrae, an optional subphylum.

Aves—the class of birds, warm-blooded, feathered, egg-laying. There are 27 or 28 orders of birds and among them 9,000 or so species.

Passeriformes—the order of perching birds. There are 5,100 species, distributed among 74 families. Three toes point forward and one points to the rear. There are no webs on the feet. Young are blind and helpless when hatched.

Estrildidae—a family or a subfamily of weavers. Estrildid weavers include waxbills, grassfinches and mannikins. Here we find zebras, Java sparrows and mannikins. Some classifiers disagree and have placed zebras in another family.

Spermestidae—another suggested name for the family of grassfinches which includes zebras and many other Australian finches.

Ploceidae—this family includes the "true" weavers, widowbirds and sparrows. Let us in this book assume that the zebra is either a Spermestidae or an Estrildid weaver rather than a Ploceid weaver. Eventually the problem will be resolved, but this is not the place.

Taeniopygia—one of the generic names currently used for the zebra finch. Note that this is one currently popular generic name, not necessarily the name for all time.

Taeni—means with a fillet or headband or ribbon and *pygia* means relative to the rump. I assume then that "ribbon rumped" refers to the narrow white rump stripe of the zebra finch. Most people would never notice it.

Guttata—the specific name. It means "with drop-like spots" and perhaps this was chosen to describe the white dots on the chestnut flanks of the male zebra finch or perhaps it refers to the white marks on tails of both sexes.

Castanotis—is another specific or subspecific name which refers to either the chestnut cheek or chestnut flank color of the male zebra finch. For a while some fanciers did call it the chestnut-eared finch, but that's past history.

Poephila—another of the generic names currently used for the zebra finch. *Poephila* means lover of grass.

Everyone knows what a zebra finch is, even if taxonomists disagree about the scientific name.

In the past 160 years this bird has had but two common English names, but let's see how the scientists have treated it.

There is some evidence that a zebra finch was exhibited in Paris in 1805, but it was not until 1817 that the record became unequivocal since it was then described scientifically and named by Viellot. Twenty years later that great explorer and naturalist, Gould, referred to it in his *Synopsis of Birds of Australia* and he called it *Amadina castanotis*. Later Gould renamed it *Taeniopygia castanotis*. Subsequently Gould was thought to be wrong and the little bird was renamed *Poephila guttata*, but this name, it turned out, was already assigned to another bird, however very closely related. So our Australian zebra finch was then relegated to subspecies rank as *Poephila guttata castanotis*, but many authors still call it *Taeniopygia guttata*. At least six names since 1837—that's not bad for a bird only four and a half inches long! So, then, in the literature you will find references to:

Fringilla guttata—Viellot 1817

Amadina castanotis—Gould (1837)

Taeniopygia guttata castanotis—Gould (after 1837)

Poephila guttata—Subsequent to Gould

Poephila guttata castanotis—Prior to Rutgers

Taeniopygia guttata—Rutgers 1964

Poephila castanotis—*Larousse Encyclopedia of Animal Life* (1967)

and all refer to the same bird, the zebra finch. Another common name adopted and later rejected by most fanciers is chestnut-eared finch. Call it a zebra and everyone will know what you are talking about. Dr. Klaus Immelmann tells us that the Germans say *Zebrafink*, the French say *Diamant mandarin* and the Dutch call it *Zebravink*.

Zebra finches are found naturally wild over 90% of the subcontinent of Australia. This is a tremendous area for one species to range and still remain homogenous. There is just this one species inhabiting all Australia excepting only some coastal forest and marshy areas in the

(1,2) These zebra pairs exhibit the basic gray, wild coloration, also called "normal." The black-and-white barred tail is distinctive and adds a lot of sparkle to a cage or aviary since these birds are usually very active.

The "zebra" markings on the male's throat are evident here. However, the bill of the female is usually lighter than that of the male, particularly when she is mature.

south, east and north. Several races within the species have been described by Mathews but these variations are not meaningful to bird-keepers.

One time-consuming diversion for writers of natural history is a study of the existing literature. Here we can find amusing and distressing contradictions deserving solution by Agatha Christie or Ellery Queen or Edgar Allan Poe. For example, Cyril Rogers in 1977 wrote a book entitled *Zebra Finches*, and in this otherwise excellent book there is a colored map showing the range of the zebra finch. Here we find the zebra on Tasmania, Sumba, Timor, and on the *coastal* parts of Australia excepting the south-central and west-central coasts. The center of the subcontinent is not inhabited by zebra finches, according to the map in Roger's book. Of course, this map is absolutely wrong.

G. W. Iles wrote a book recently which is not dated. It is entitled *Breeding Australian Finches*, published by Isles d'Avon Ltd. In this book we find a map with shaded areas which show the same zebra finch inhabiting the same islands of Timor and Sumba as in Rogers', but not Tasmania (there are over 26,000 square miles in Tasmania). Furthermore, on his map of Australia, Iles correctly and accurately indicates that zebra finches inhabit the entire interior (approximately two million square miles) and most of the west coast, but he has no zebras on virtually all of the remaining *coastal* land that they occupy according to Cyril Rogers' map. Most interestingly, Iles' accurate map and Rogers' text are in very close agreement.

To the north of Australia and southwest of New Guinea lie the islands of the Lesser Sundas, Flores, Sumba and Timor and it was here that the aforementioned *Poephila guttata* (also sometimes called *Taeniopygia guttata guttata)* was found. This subspecies is not domesticated to the degree that the Australian zebra is, but it has been imported and exhibited from time to time. These birds are larger than our caged zebras and the colors are darker. The bars on throat and breast are less pronounced. Some authorities designate it *Poephila guttata*, a wild subspecies of the native species of Australia, sometimes called *Taeniopygia guttata*. Obviously the nomenclature is wrong; both should be either in the genus *Poephila* or genus *Taeniopygia* and subspecific (trinomial) names should be assigned.

Taeniopygia will probably lose out to *Poephila* in this situation because *Poephila* seems to be the earlier designation. The word *Poephila* is reasonable for the zebra finch. Grass lover is really a good generic name for a little finch that builds grass nests and eats grass seeds.

WILD ZEBRAS

All of Australia (except some coastal and tropical forested areas) is

The fluffing of the male is typical after bathing or, more probably, in the course of preening by his mate.

home to the zebra, and this makes it as common a sight as the English (or house) sparrow is in the U.S.A. The wild Australian zebra finch looks much like our gray (or normal) domesticated zebra except that wild birds are said to have reddish eyes while the domesticated strain has brown eyes.

Dr. Klaus Immelmann suggests that the various populations of this vast continent are not differentiated into subspecies because the periodic droughts force the birds to move into new areas from time to time and this causes the various stocks to interbreed. He goes on to tell us that this most common bird adapts to a variety of wild habitats. Additionally, it does well near people. As a result colonies of birds build up near water tanks and cattle watering troughs. It is also found, he says, near houses, orchards, gardens, cultivated fields and pastures.

They need water for drinking and bathing, so the native bushmen regard them as a good sign of water nearby. Their food in the wild is reported to be half-ripe and ripe grass seed. Poa-grass is a favored food. Incidentally, Kentucky blue grass is also in this genus of Poa grasses. Additionally, wild zebras eat insects. Flying termites and fly pupae are eaten avidly by wild Australian zebra finches.

The Australian government has banned the export of its finches, and perhaps all other birds as well, but this does not adversely affect the zebra finch hobby throughout the world since there is plenty of genetic material available in the birds held in captivity all over the rest of the world.

17

(1,2) A gray penguin male (3,4) A fawn penguin male—note how dilute the fawn color is in this specimen.

(1,2) A gray penguin female. (3,4) A fawn penguin female.

Left: In this pair of adult zebras, the female has the typical tear marks under her eyes, but she lacks the cheek, breast and flank markings. **Below:** Natural twigs make great perches because there is variety in diameter and springiness. When they get dirty, just replace them with new branches.

Zebra Behavior

Let's look at a large cage or aviary of zebras and make a list of the things that we should expect normal healthy zebras to do.

Action. They will be active most of the daytime. They will flitter and twitter and preen themselves and each other. Adults will feed the juveniles and juveniles will screech for food as though they were starving. There will be some quiet periods during the daylight hours. The birds will then perch singly or in small groups and snooze or just look around. These rest periods might last as long as a half-hour.

Bathing. Zebras will bathe daily or even twice daily. They will prefer to do this when the sun is bright, and after a moment of shaking off the loose water, they will dry and preen in direct sunlight.

Eating. Zebras will eat on and off all day. They will slack off about an hour before they go to roost for the night.

1

2

(1) The color dilution that characterizes many zebra mutations appears in this cream male. (2) A female zebra photographed in the wild. (3) A chestnut-flanked white pair. Compare with cream male (1).

Roosting. They seem to crave a closed place to sleep at night. Pairs will often roost together in their nest with their eggs or fledglings or in a spare nest if the fledglings are so large as to use up all the room.

Noises. No one, however much he likes zebras, can call the birds melodious—they make a great volume and variety of noises that seem to mean something to each other. This goes on all during the daylight hours. There is variety to the sounds they make. Fledglings scream for food and adults chirp or squeak. No bird keeper would own a zebra finch simply to enjoy its song. Happy, healthy zebras are not silent.

Territories. They do stake out claims for territory in and around their nests but unless you crowd them, there is not any serious bullying around the feeder or the water.

Pair Bonds. They seem to form long-lasting or perhaps permanent pair bonds. If one of a pair dies, the other will re-mate, maybe not tomorrow, but soon.

Curiosity. Zebras are full of it. One would have to go to crows or hookbills (parrots and parrot-like birds) to find more inquisitive birds. If you put any device in a cage, they will be on it and, if possible, in it within minutes.

Reproduction. They are quite sexy. During their waking hours (unless they are resting, eating, bathing, feeding their young or preening) the chances are good that what they are doing somehow relates to reproduction. Nesting materials will be collected. Nest sites will be explored. Males will court their mates. Nests will be constructed. This is a big thing with healthy normal zebras—twelve months of the year.

Molting. There will be no dramatic molting of plumage among healthy normal zebra finches. They will look the same all year long. When they do molt it will be just a few feathers at a time and no bird will ever look especially patchy. Even the juvenile, as it matures, will develop adult coloration gradually.

A heavy molt is a sign that your birds are ill or that you have made a sudden (and ill-advised) environmental change. If this should happen, be sure that your birds are amply furnished with a wide variety of food supplements and that they are protected from drafts. Bear in mind that healthy zebras will thrive in unheated aviaries if they have warm draft-free roosts and plenty of proper food, including oily seeds. They can even survive some intermittent intense cold if not subjected to wetness or draft.

The birds in my aviary voluntarily and avidly go out of doors every day of the year—and this is in New England!

Sociability. Zebra finches get along well with other birds. They also get along well with people. A zebra will not likely become as intimate with you as a parrot but it certainly will get to recognize you and perhaps even land on your finger or shoulder.

Another social aspect of the zebra finch fancy is that it brings people together. People will visit you to see your birds and you will visit them to see theirs. You will go to shows, join a club, subscribe to a magazine, write letters and easily become involved in a great hobby.

Hardiness. Zebras are tough. They will even thrive in an aviary where their drinking water is frozen every morning, so long as you provide them with a couple of chances to drink every day. They will live for years without disease. The only handling some may need is an occasional nail clipping. In my experience, zebra finches are tougher than society finches or budgies or canaries.

THE PECKING ORDER

Chickens are famous for their henhouse and barnyard pecking orders, and psychologists have climbed the ladder of academic acclaim by writing papers about these pecking orders. It goes on everywhere, all the time.

When the pecking order syndrome is applied to zebra finches, you will discover that a single pair does well together. Three or four pairs stimulate each other to breed more frequently BUT with two pairs or an odd bird in a small group, you may experience trouble.

A simplistic explanation is that zebras cannot count too much over four or five. A cage or an aviary with a half dozen birds will not have a pecked or picked-on bird on the bottom of the ladder because no other bird remembers which is which.

I'm reminded of the dreaded piranha of the Amazon River which when kept in an aquarium must be solitary since it will destroy or be destroyed. There was for many years a display tank in the Shedd Aquarium, Chicago with three or four dozen of these fish. Even though (now and then) one might get nipped, there was no widespread mayhem. If, however, the fish were separated into groups of perhaps three, the results would surely be fatally bloody.

So, keep a pair or keep a half-dozen or more birds, but avoid some number in between.

CROWDING

All of us know that many creatures are social. There are butterflies that migrate together and snakes that hibernate together and whales that swim together and wolves that run in packs together, and bats that hang in their caves together. Zebra finches do it too, but this doesn't mean that you can pack them in a cage or an aviary as the Portuguese pack sar-

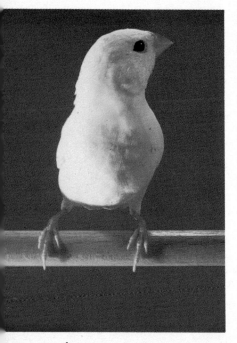

4

(1,2) A white zebra hen. (3) One of these zebras has a ragged tail, and the other is squatting on its perch. Neither should be entered in a show. (4) This gray male is almost perfect, but show standards may require that he be banded.

1

2

3

(1,2,3) A zebra fledgling is being fed by its mother. This usually happens for two or three weeks until the little fellows become independent.

dines. In other words, just because they get along well with each other they should not be thoughtlessly crowded.

For one thing, the risk of loss from communicable disease is ever present, and it increases as the population increases. Then too there is the matter of territories. Watch the few birds you have. Each will favor a particular perch, a special position in the bath, the same roosting place every night, a nest site. This is their life!

For a rule of thumb, give each caged bird one square foot of floor space. In an aviary, you might squeeze three birds into every two square feet, but that's the practical limit.

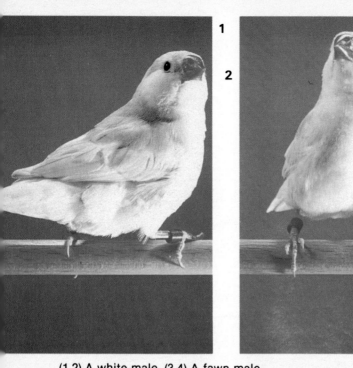

(1,2) A white male. (3,4) A fawn male.

(1,2) A white female. (3,4) A fawn female.

Left: The flecking that sometimes appears on the back of white zebras is apparent on this bird. **Below:** The pied factor appears in the center pair of zebras.

Colors

This chapter is sticky because the names of the colors and patterns are not universally accepted, because new colors and patterns are being developed all the time, and because the genetic principles that apply are not necessarily fully known. The companion book to this one is entitled *Breeding Zebra Finches;* there the genetics are explained in some detail. For the final, authoritative word on colors, you should read the Zebra Finch Society standards, which are the same for Britain and the United States. Afterwards, I'll review briefly the many and overlapping names of the established colors.

STANDARDS OF THE ZEBRA FINCH SOCIETY
(Reprinted with their kind permission)
SHOW STANDARDS

CONDITION to be essential. Birds should not receive any award

unless in perfect show condition. (Missing, ragged or soiled feathers, and missing claws or toes constitute show faults).

TYPE. Bold throughout and of the "Cobby" type, giving the birds a look of substance; wings evenly carried to root of tail.

MARKINGS (COCKS). Chest bar distinct and clear cut, *not less* than 1/8 in. wide and of even width throughout. Side flankings should be prominent, extending from wing butts to end of rump and decorated with round, clearly defined white spots. Beak coral red with feet and legs deep pink. All markings where applicable to be clear and distinct. Hens as for cocks less cheek patches, chest bar and side flankings; beak a paler shade of red. Male markings on hens are definite show faults.

COLOUR STANDARDS

NORMAL COCK. Eyes dark. Beak red. Feet and legs red. Head and neck dark grey, wings grey. Breast bar jet black. Throat and upper breast zebra striped, grey with darker lines running from cheek to cheek continuing down to chest bar. Underparts white, may have some fawnish shading near vent and thighs. Cheek lobes dark orange. Tear markings black and distinct. Tail, black with white bars, side flankings reddish brown with clear white spots.

HEN. As for cock minus chest barring, lobe and flank markings. Beak paler in colour. Tear markings black and distinct. A lighter shade of normal is recognised.

Show faults: Brown shading on wings and mantle.

WHITE, COCK AND HEN. Eyes dark. Beak red. Feet and legs pink. Pure white all over. Hens usually have beaks of a paler shade of red.

Show faults: Coloured spangles on mantle.

FAWN COCK. Eyes dark. Beak red. Feet and legs pink. Head, neck and wings deep even fawn. Breast bar dark. Throat and upper breast light fawn with zebra lines running from cheek to cheek continuing down to breast bar. Underparts white, may have some fawnish shading near vent and thighs, cheek lobes dark orange, tear markings same shade as breast bar. Tail dark barred with white. Side flankings reddish brown with even clear white spots.

HEN. As other hens but of the same shade of fawn as cocks.

Show faults: Variation in colour between cock and hen or pairs.

DOMINANT SILVER (DILUTE NORMAL) COCK. Eyes dark. Beak red. Feet and legs pink. There are various shades of dilute normals, silvery grey being the ideal. Chest bars vary from sooty to pale grey, cheek lobes vary from pale orange to pale cream, flanking from reddish to pinkish fawn with even clear white spots. Tear markings same shade as breast bar. The lighter the general colour the paler the chest, tail lobe and flankings. Tail dark with white bars.

HEN. As other hens but of the same shade to match the cocks.

Show faults: Variation in colour between cock and hen of pairs and variation in colour of individual birds. Fawn shadings. Indistinct markings on cocks.

DOMINANT CREAM (DILUTE FAWN) COCK. Eyes dark. Beak red. Feet and legs pink. Again all shades from deep cream to pale cream. Markings in cocks to be in general tone to match depth of diluteness. Tear markings same shade as breast bar. Tail deep cream with white bars.

HEN. As other hens but of the same shade to match the cocks.

Show faults: Variation in colour between cock and hen of pairs and variation in colour of individual birds. Fawn shadings. Indistinct markings on cocks.

PIED COCK AND HEN. Eyes dark. Beak red, feet and legs pink. Any other colours broken with white approximately 50% of each colour (white underparts not to be included in this 50%). Cock to retain cock markings in broken form on cheeks, flanks and chest. Tear markings distinct but can be broken.

Show faults: Loss of cock markings which should be shown in broken form. Exhibition pairs to be matched for Pied markings.

CHESTNUT FLANKED WHITE COCK. Eyes dark, beak red. Feet and legs pink. Head, neck, back and wings as white as possible. Underparts pure white. Breast bar as near black as possible. Tear markings same shade as breast bar. Cheek lobes orange. Tail white with bars. Colour to match chest bar. Flank markings reddish brown with clear white spots.

HEN. As other hens to match cocks. May have light head markings.

Show faults: Markings too pale in the cock.

PENGUIN (NORMAL) COCK. Eyes dark. Beak red. Feet and legs pink. Head, neck and wings a light even silver grey, with flights, secondaries and coverts edged with a paler shade of grey giving a laced effect. (This lacing does not show to full advantage until the second full moult.) Underparts from beak to vent pure white without any trace of barring. Cheek lobes pale orange to pale cream to match body colour of bird. Tail silvery grey barred with white. Side flankings reddish brown with clear white spots.

HEN. As other hens but with cheek lobes white.

(There can be Penguin forms of the other colours.)

Show faults: Barring on chest.

RECESSIVE SILVER (DILUTE NORMAL) COCK. Eyes dark. Beak red. Feet and legs pink. Head, neck and mantle medium bluish grey, wings grey. Throat and upper breast zebra striped, bluish grey with darker lines running from cheek to cheek continuing down to chest bar. Chest bar dark grey. Tear marks distinct and to match colour of chest bar. Cheek lobes medium orange. Underparts white sometimes slightly shaded near thighs and vent. Flankings light reddish brown with clear white spots. Tail dark with white bars. Cock markings should be clear and distinct with only slight dilution.

HEN. As other hens but of the same shade to match the cocks.

Show faults: Variation in colour between cock and hen of pairs and variation in colour of individual birds. Fawn shadings. Indistinct markings on cock. Colour too dark or too light.

RECESSIVE CREAM (DILUTE FAWN) COCK. Eyes dark. Beak red. Feet and legs pink. Head, neck and mantle medium cream, wings cream. Throat and upper breast zebra striped, cream with darker lines running from cheek to cheek continuing down to chest bar. Cheek lobes medium orange. Underparts white sometimes slightly shaded near thighs and vent. Flankings light reddish brown with clear white spots. Tail dark cream with white bars. Cock markings should be clear and distinct with only slight dilution.

HEN. As other hens but of the same shade to match the cocks.

Show faults: Variation in colour between cock and hen of pairs and variation in colour of individual birds. Fawn shadings. Indistinct markings on cocks. Colours too dark or too light.

YELLOW-BEAKED VARIETIES. General colouring as Normal Grey and all other mutations except the beak which should be shades of yellow with the cock birds showing the richest colour. There can be a Yellow-beaked form of all existing mutations and their composite forms. Yellow-beaks must be exhibited in true pairs of the same mutation.

Show faults: As with the normal red-beaked kinds.

A.O.C. In the interest of breeders and exhibitors no new colour will be recognised until thoroughly investigated by the Committee.

Panel Judges are reminded that the Show and Colour Standards must be observed. Zebra Finches can only be shown in true pairs, i.e., a cock and a hen at Patronage Shows. A pair must always consist of two birds of the same mutation.

This unusual zebra finch appears to be bisexed. One side has the markings of a male, while the other is like the female.

THE ZEBRA FINCH SOCIETY STANDARD SHOW CAGE

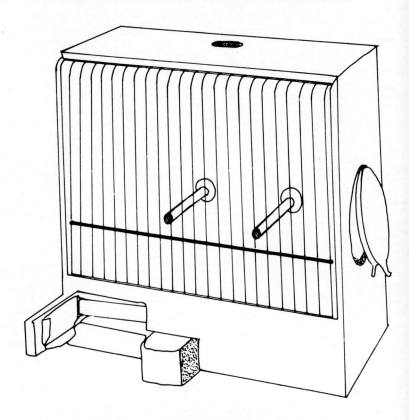

SPECIFICATION

SIZE. Overall measurement: 12" long, 11¼" high, 6" wide.

WOOD. Top, sides and false roof. Back good quality 4mm. ply.

DOOR. Round 3½" dia. centre 5.3/8" from floor of cage, 2.7/8" from sides, one wire loop.

FRONT RAIL. Height 2.3/8" from floor, turn out feeder door on left hand side of front rail 3½" long by 1.3/8" deep; sloping cut at edge. 16-gauge escape bar fixed to door. Door fastened by 7/8" brass desk turn painted black. Zinc clip screwed to inside of door to carry white plastic drinker, ¾" 16-gauge S-hook on outside.

PERCHES. Length 4" overall measured from the back of the cage, 3/8" diameter with plain boss at back 1" diameter projecting 3/8". Perches to be fixed 4.3/8" from floor of cage and 4" apart on the centre line of the cage horizontally.

WIRE FRONT. Comprising 23 wires, 16-gauge mesh, ½" centre to centre, double punched bar at top set 3/16" apart, for fixing two wires left at top and bottom.

TOP. Width 5¼". Carrying hole 1¼" dia., centre 1¾" from back of cage.

COLOUR. Inside painted white, outside and wire front black.

Floor Covering– Any millet or mixture suitable for Zebras.

NO MAKERS NAME TO APPEAR ON CAGE

THE ZEBRA FINCH SOCIETY STANDARD SHOW CAGE

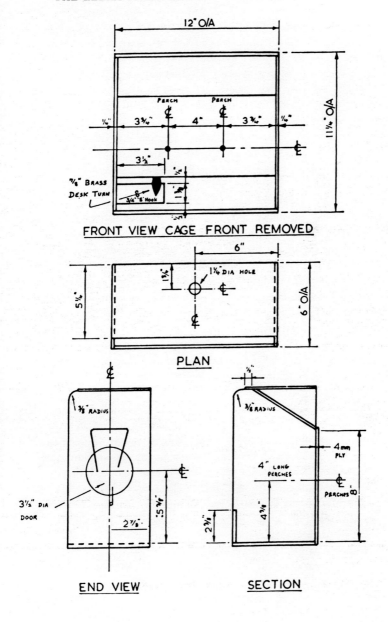

FRONT VIEW CAGE FRONT REMOVED

PLAN

END VIEW

SECTION

COLOR COMMENTS

Gray, normal wild. This color resembles the wild Australian zebra finch for all intents and purposes. Some see it as a bit brownish or a bit more or less ashy brown, but since Mathews described several races of wild birds, we will quickly get into some pretty involved circumlocution. Suffice it to say a gray must not have any irregular white feathers.

Gray is easy but few people can agree very long on the names of various other colors. Cyril H. Rogers, author of the *Encyclopedia of Cage and Aviary Birds,* an aviculturist for over forty years and 1978 President of the Zebra Finch Society (British) has this to say in the August 1978 Society Newsletter: "It is interesting to note that early Fawns were known as Cinnamons but the Dilute forms were always known as Creams. The name Fawn was apparently given to both Cinnamons when they were light and also to certain Silvers that showed a brownish shading above." Not only *interesting* but difficult, especially if all the books a fancier owns were not written at the same time.

Incidentally, this bird which Cyril Rogers discusses is also sometimes called a fawn-brown or an Isabel. When you get to be an expert you too can coin a name or two. I advise you not to take these names too seriously as you get started in this hobby. The bird is so subtly variable in color it almost defies a simple description. Even the best color photos leave something to be desired.

One popular color pattern with several names is the absence of black. The male lacks any belly or breast markings. Call it a white throated or silverwing or penguin. The basic color will be diluted as well.

There are plenty of all-white zebra finches in pet shops and fanciers' cages, but at the time of this writing, none have pink eyes. Some have ruby red eyes and some have brownish red eyes or reddish brown eyes. Now the convention among students of genetics is to describe an albino as an individual which lacks all color pigment. The albino mouse is a good example. It has white hair and its eyes are not red; they are pink. Using the pink eye criterion, the 1980 white, red-eyed zebra finch is technically not an absolutely true albino. Dr. Matthew M. Vriends in his *Handbook of Zebra Finches* points this out and he chooses to call these birds pseudo-albino.

I look at nature in another way. I find few absolutes anywhere. Most living forms are literally and figuratively shades of gray. Therefore I call the red-eyed white an albino. I don't argue with Dr. Vriends; I simply see it differently and this is my book.

Some people have reported that there are blue zebra finches. Well, maybe. We already know that some (or perhaps all) black specimens are that way because of a dietary deficiency. Increase of vitamin D will result in lighter colors with their next set of feathers.

We also know that some bird exporters in the Orient have been coloring their birds with dyes, with sprays or baths for years. Canaries in Europe and the U.S.A. are sometimes fed on red foods so as to subsequently sprout reddish feathers.

Don't invest your life's savings in a breeding pair of purple zebra finches; they might just turn white or gray after their first molt.

Another group of color and pattern arrangements comes from hybrids. Since about two dozen related species have been hybridized with captive zebra finches, one can hardly imagine all the color and pattern combinations and permutations that are possible. Some are really beautiful. Most are sterile.

The gray wild natural zebra finch has surely produced color and feathering mutations in nature which made their bearers more conspicuous and vulnerable to attack by predators. These same mutations occur on a chance basis in the nests of cage birds as well, and here is where the bird keeper (with the help of Gregor Mendel and other geneticists) establishes new color varieties. The "feathering" I alluded to is a crest or crown or rosette of feathers on the top of the head. There are plenty of crested zebras in the hands of fanciers, but they don't stir up much excitement.

The progenitors of variously colored zebras may not have been perfectly pigmented but rather they were possibly light-colored birds and/or grays with but one or two light colored feathers. By thoughtful selective breeding, fanciers picked the birds which were mostly the desired color, and by inbreeding for this characteristic they finally achieved a pure (true breeding) strain. This is no "big deal." With most characteristics like this, it is just hard work for about fifty years. This is not long when we look at the time and effort that has gone into Jersey cattle, Percheron horses, Cocker Spaniels, Leghorn chickens, Siamese cats, Big Boy tomatoes or American Beauty roses.

Zebra varieties are not locked in, nor are they the sole property or privilege of any person or group of people. New colors or patterns crop up all over the birdkeeping world and you can, given the time and patience and a little understanding of genetic principles, "create" a distinctively different zebra finch. This is done in the same way that Henry Wallace "created" new varieties of corn or Paul Hahnel and Bill Sternke and Myron Gordon "created" new varieties of fish.

Actually man does not "create" these life forms. All he does is to use his God-given intelligence to sort out genetic material which mutated spontaneously or was latent for ages as a recessive trait and which simply required selective breeding to make it evident.

Left: Two eggs of the clutch have been laid. The zealous parents have provided a covering for the nest, as in the wild. **Below:** These squeakers need several more days before they will be out of the nest.

Life Cycle

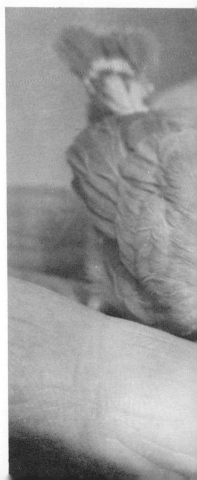

My companion book titled *Breeding Zebra Finches* covers this aspect in detail but here is a brief review. You may note that there are few things they always do and a few things they never do and many things they *may* do; their life style permits some rule-bending.

Zebras are social birds. They travel in small flocks and nest near each other. The nest is frequently in a low shrub and it looks untidy outside. The twigs and coarse grass stems are woven somewhat but it is not neat outside as is a Baltimore oriole's. Inside, it is lined with soft material; feathers, wool, vegetable down and soft grass are all commonly employed. The usual clutch consists of four white eggs. The eggs will hatch about two weeks after they were laid.

Both parents will spend the night in the nest. Zebras will sometimes build a nest to raise young and then build a second nest for roosting at night. They seem to prefer to roost in protected places.

This cock is in fine plumage: his feathers are clean and tight.

The young will breed when they are hardly more than two months out of the nest. This is generally considered by aviculturists to be poor practice and so they separate the sexes to prevent the breeding of immature birds.

It would be very difficult for a person to estimate accurately the age of a zebra finch from the time it is six months old until it dies of old age, perhaps six or ten or even twelve years later.

SEX RECOGNITION

Female zebras probably identify males by how they behave since even all-white males seem to have no trouble finding mates. All-white (self-whites), silvers and white pseudo-albino males have more red color in their bills than do the females—and that is the only difference apparent to people.

The normal "wild" gray and many of the other color varieties show sexual differences (dimorphism) as follows:

Male	*Female*
Orange cheekpiece	Gray or basic body color
Striped throat and upper chest	Gray or pale basic body color
Lower chest bears a horizontal black bar one-eighth inch wide	Lower chest same as basic body color
Dark coral-red beak	Paler orange-red beak
Flanks—chestnut, with round white spots	Flanks—pale, same as basic breast color, unspotted

Juveniles, for the first 8 or 10 weeks after leaving the nest, look like females except that their bills are brown-black and gradually become coral or orange as they mature.

In the nest, juveniles are quite hairy or fuzzy and when the nest is lined with feathers (as is often the case), the newly hatched birds are frequently indistinguishable from their bedding.

Eggs of domestic birds are smooth, white and slightly chalky. They are slightly larger at one end, much in the manner of an ordinary hen's egg. No one has suggested a way to determine the sex of an unhatched chick. I'm not sure anyone cares.

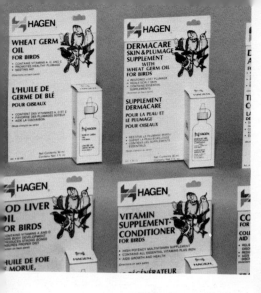

Left and below: There are many fine products for birds available at your pet shop.

Nutrition Water and Bathing

Zebra finch diet is simple, but the basics must be available. No zebra can live on peanut butter and lettuce alone—however he may enjoy these things. The basic diet is the seed of a grass, millet seed. Remember that one of the zebra's various generic names is *Poephila,* the lover of grass. There are several varieties, colors and sizes of millet in the marketplace and you may find that the best source of grain is your pet shop where you can obtain one-pound cartons of a "finch mixture". This consists of mostly millet with canary, rape, niger, oats and perhaps still other grains. If you have more than thirty birds, one-pound packages will not suffice; you should be getting your millet or finch mixture in bulk—perhaps 25 pounds or even 50 pounds at a time.

Which millet should you feed zebra finches? Try a few and settle for the one or two they favor. The nutrient values of all millets are about

An alternative to buying and mixing your own seeds is to purchase
mixtures specially prepared for finches.

the same. The sizes and colors vary. Most of the color in millet is in the
husk and your bird will remove the millet husk before he eats the grain
anyway. Don't take millet color too seriously.

Buy clean grain—not damp, not water-stained, not moldy. It may
have some webs in it, and if you watch patiently, you may see movement. Not quite as much as the movement of Mexican jumping beans,
but movement nevertheless. The webs and the movement mean that
there are little soft white or creamy colored grubs in your birdseed.
These grubs are perhaps as large around as a pencil lead and they will
grow to about five-eighths of an inch long. A grub of a web-moth has a
cylindrical body with two rows of legs—much like a tiny inch-worm, except that they don't "inch," they simply creep about in the grain. Later,
the grubs will pupate in cocoons and small moths will emerge to continue their cycle of life. Your zebra finches may or may not eat the white
web "worms" in the grain. Some aviculturists report that they do, and
others report that they do not touch any insects. No harm in trying. If
they do eat the web "worms", then offer them mealworms too.

You should test your grain to assure that it is alive. The viability of
millet is much more important to your birds than is its color. Plant
some as you would grass seed or put some on a wet towel for a few days

to be sure that at least 75% of it germinates; that is, sprouts. Incidentally, your birds will enjoy eating sprouted grain as a diet supplement.

Although millet is the basic diet ingredient for seed-eating finches, its protein content is lower than what breeding and baby finches ideally should have. One problem is that millet lacks certain amino acids. This is why experienced bird keepers will offer a variety of oily seeds including rape, niger, poppy and sesame to supplement the basic millet diet. In case you wondered why oily seeds are recommended to increase protein in the diet, it is a fact that most high-fat seeds are also high in protein. Canary seed, a notable exception, is a good protein source even though it is not relatively high in oil.

Interestingly, canary seed, *Phalaris canariensis,* happens to be high in those amino acids which are correspondingly low in millet, *Panicum miliaceum.* It should also be mentioned here that spray millet is in fact not a *Panicum* but is classified in another genus of plants and is scientifically called *Setaria italica.*

One pitfall experienced by many beginning finch keepers is that of husks versus seeds. These birds don't carry whole seeds in their bills and they don't swallow them either. When a zebra finch picks up a grain of canary seed or a grain of millet, it positions and holds the grain between the upper and lower bill using its tongue to manipulate it. A squeeze or two pops the husk off in one or two parts and then the husked seed is swallowed. The husk then falls aside within an inch of the place it was picked up. Soon the seed dispenser or dish is full of inedible chaff and the birds could be starving. If your eyes are not sharp enough to discriminate between whole grain and husks, you might try blowing at the food dish—the chaff will be much lighter and since it is cup-shaped, it will tend to be caught in the airstream and carried off. If you keep several hundred birds you should buy a winnower; it will pay for itself in saved grain and you can give up the blowing.

An alternative to winnowing is simply to dump the chaff-laden grain into a tray of moistened earth where the chaff will become mulch and much of the remaining grain will sprout. Your birds will then consume in sprouted form what would otherwise be lost.

The following table gives the average values for most of the foods your finches will eat. Notice that canary seed is unusually high in minerals (ash), but also be aware that these figures will vary with the soil in which the plants are growing, the rainfall and the maturity of the seeds when they were harvested. The bird seed business is well established and highly competitive. Generally, you get what you pay for.

| Foodstuff | Percentage of: | | | | Carbo- |
	Protein	Fat	Fiber	Ash	hydrate*
Egg (White)	10	1	0	1	0
Egg (Yolk)	15	24	0	1	0
Bread	16	2	2	2	70
Peanut Butter	30	40	3	2	15
Rice	8	2	9	5	65
Millet	13	2	9	4	62
Canary Seed	14	4	21	10	27
Spray Millet	15	6	11	6	51
Sunflower	15	28	29	3	17
Fennel	16	12	14	9	32
Niger	19	43	14	3	12
Rape	20	45	6	4	18
Caraway	20	17	16	7	29
Poppy	21	50	5	7	10
Sesame	21	47	5	6	19
Hemp	22	30	19	5	16
Gold of Pleasure	22	31	11	7	22
Flax	24	37	6	4	22
Green Vegetables	10	3	25	1	20

(mostly leafy; varies greatly with moisture)
*Carbohydrate, other than fiber

It has been suggested that the protein for seed eating finches should be about 19% of the diet. Actually when the bird shucks the husk from millet, its fiber content will go down several percentage points and therefore protein will increase somewhat from the figures shown here but even so these figures still explain why experienced breeders will offer more than just millet to their birds.

SPRAY MILLET

There is no shortage of bird fanciers who are willing to buy spray millet for their birds at more than two dollars per pound, and in small quantities they will pay as much as three dollars a pound! They know that their birds love it.

Release your birds in a large sunny aviary and let them settle down. Some will bathe, others roost, still others will pick at grit, preen, build nests or simply fly back and forth. There will be little or no uniform activity, especially if there are several species present. Then put a few stalks of spray millet in a weighted vase or hang a bundle from a wire

(1) This is spray millet, an excellent treat for all finches. A dozen birds will demolish this in just a few days. (2) Dice up an egg boiled for thirty minutes and put the shell back in with it. Zebra finches love the whole thing.

and within minutes *all* the birds of *all* the species will be picking over that millet.

If you have trouble with that over-two-dollars-per-pound price tag, you might try a late summer walk through a field. With a shopping bag and a pair of snippers you can gather all sorts of weeds that are going to seed. If you want to be scientific about it you should read two paperback Dover reprints:

Martin, Zim and Nelson, *American Wildlife and Plants,* New York, 1961.

Knobel, Edward, *Field Guide to the Grasses, Sedges and Rushes of the U.S.,* New York, 1977.

Both of these books point out that spray millet or foxtail millet or bristlegrass or *Setaria italica* is the same species whether domesticated or wild. If you purchase a domestic farm grown product, you have the right to assume that it was not treated with any dangerous insecticide and of course if you harvest it from a field, you should know whether that field had been sprayed. Not likely, since no one wastes expensive sprays on weed fields. More importantly, cultivated millet tends to have larger seeds. The choice is up to you; regardless, the response from the birds will justify your expense or your effort.

FOOD SUPPLEMENTS

Among the supplements which your zebras may enjoy are honey and oranges. You might offer a slice of bread or toast moistened with a mixture of honey and orange juice or perhaps just one or the other.

Powdered yeast will stick to grain which was moistened with cod liver oil and this is a high fat, high protein, high vitamin D supplement which your birds could well be given occasionally.

Although, and this bears repeating, zebra finches can live out normal lives with minerals, grit, water and millet, this is much like a jailbird limited to bread and water. He will survive. Period.

So, sweeten the pot with green foods such as lettuce, spinach and celery tops, the supplements already mentioned, thirty minute hard-boiled eggs whole (with shells removed) or diced up with a fork or pushed through a strainer. Also offer foods derived from insects. Termites and silkworm pupae are nutritionally excellent but a bother to prepare. You can buy them from your pet dealer or through advertisements in the bird magazines. Don't stock a big inventory of insectile food until you test a little of it. Your zebras may refuse to touch it, but if insect-eating birds are with the zebras in the same cage or aviary, your birds may learn to eat this high protein food as a supplement after watching the others do it.

Still another food supplement from which your zebras might benefit is dried seaweed. This is high in minerals and they may have a craving for it if a trace element is otherwise lacking in their diet.

As you read this book you may feel "snowed" by all the remarks about what zebra finches will eat. Really it isn't mandatory that you feed each item every day. The supplements are mostly optional. Your birds will survive and thrive and even breed on a diet of water, millet, grit, minerals and a little green food from time to time. As I mentioned previously, treats such as French toast and milk sop are like the frosting on the cake. One can manage without them but life is better when they are included.

Other more delicate cage bird species might not even survive without some supplements to the basic grain diet—for them these foods are not supplements; they are an integral part of the regular diet. On the other hand, the hardy zebra likes the supplements, does better for them, but does not require them for survival.

During the course of writing and illustrating this book, an eight by twelve foot inside aviary with a connected three foot by six foot outside flight cage was home to about thirty zebra finches. They multiplied to the point where some were removed to avoid crowding. These birds were fed just once every 24 hours. The one dish for bath and drinking water was changed daily and about a cup of mixed canary seed and millet replaced the husks left from the previous day. About ¼ cup of soaked grain (canary and millet) "started" the previous morning was also offered sometimes. Additionally, one quarter to one half a hard-boiled chicken egg (sometimes broken up with a fork) *and* its crushed shell went into the aviary along with a leaf or two of green lettuce.

You might have noticed that I hedged a bit when I got to the fixing of the hard boiled egg. As a matter of fact, a whole (but shelled) hard boiled hen's egg will be eaten by zebra finches regardless of whether you chop it, dice it, sieve it or simply take off the shell and serve it whole. And when you serve it "whole" you may discover as I did that your finches prefer the white over the yolk.

The total time required to accomplish this feeding, including washing of utensils was about ten minutes. If the same number of birds were caged as pairs, the time required would be more like the better part of an hour, daily.

GRAIN AND WATER STORAGE

If you store more than a pound of grain and if mice, web-worms, mealworms or other vermin are a nuisance, consider the plastic gallon milk container. It is free, easy to clean, easy to fill by the use of a funnel,

Two good sources of minerals and trace elements are cuttlebone and mineral blocks or grit (gravel).

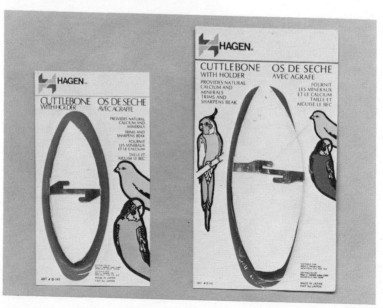

and easy to seal. With it, moisture content and loss to insects will be under your control. A label with the description and source of the seed is easy to affix; additionally, you can quickly judge how much you have on hand. Don't store grain in bright sunlight; the ultra-violet rays will degrade the nutrient values.

These narrow-necked bottles are also handy for water if you have no plumbing in your aviary or bird room. An open bucket is an invitation to disaster by drowning. Just rinse the bottles thoroughly and don't neglect to wash and screw down the caps.

MINERALS

One problem for beginning bird keepers is that they neglect the few mandatory and vital things because it all looks so simple. A good example of this oversight is neglect of your birds' mineral requirements. No zebra can survive for long without minerals, but some individuals are able to go for long periods without *ingesting* any. If the missing substance is critical, the existing supply stored in bones or blood or certain organs will be gradually depleted and the loss to the bird will take place so insidiously that you may never realize that sterility or poor plumage or death is imminent. The classic example of this is with the horse which was gradually trained to eat 100% pure sawdust. The trouble was that he dropped dead just when it looked like the experiment was a success. Your birds should have a mineral block or mineral grit mixture before them at all times. It should be situated so that it is accessible but so that it will not be covered with droppings. There is no need for you to make up this mineral mixture—there are plenty of good ones available from pet shops and cage bird supply houses. The major ingredients are sodium chloride (common salt—$NaCl$) and calcium carbonate (limestone—$CaCO_3$). The other ingredients are present as traces and include iron, copper, potassium, phosphorus, sulphur, iodine and even that notorious poison, arsenic. All animal life, man included, requires virtually all the chemically reactive elements in carefully proportioned traces. Some will come from the grain and some will be found in water, vegetables, eggs or bread or other food supplements you provide, and some may not be there. The mineral block or grit is your insurance policy. Don't neglect it. Cuttlebone is both a beak sharpener and a source of calcium plus other important trace elements but cuttlebone is not a substitute for a good mineral block or grit properly proportioned to supply all the minerals and trace elements your bird needs.

Lime can come from whole or crushed cuttlebone, crushed oyster shells, crushed lime plaster out of a very *old* house or crushed boiled or baked chicken egg shells. Most newer homes are plastered or wallboarded with gypsum plaster or gypsum wallboard (calcium sulphate), but one hundred years ago hydrated lime was used for plastering. Hydrated lime became lime carbonate over the course of time and this mineral carbonate is what you should provide to your birds. Mineral grit put up especially for cage birds surely contains this chemical compound as well as traces of everything else that birds are known to require.

One reason cuttlefish bone is so highly regarded by experienced bird-keepers is to be seen in the following figures:

Eggshell of domestic chicken—85% calcium carbonate—1.4% magnesium carbonate

Cuttlefish bone—85% calcium carbonate—.5% magnesium carbonate

The reason for the word "crushed" in a previous paragraph is that some fanciers believe that a finch cannot satisfy its need for calcium by picking at large pieces of hard material. This is, of course, true if you offer a large block of marble statuary or limestone building block, or even the shell of a cherrystone clam. Cuttlebone by contrast is so soft you can cut it with your fingernail; your zebras will have no trouble picking particles from the edges or soft side. Notice that every piece of cuttlebone does have a hard side and a soft side; if you hang it against a wall, expose the soft side. So, crush the stone and do whatever you think is right with the cuttlebone.

You may discover that the broken shells of those hard-boiled eggs you feed to your birds are favored over cuttlebone. This is great, so long as the shells were boiled for at least ½ hour—or baked over low heat in the oven. The reason is that some avian diseases are transmitted by way of raw eggs. A second reason is that it is not a good idea to suggest to a bird that raw birds' eggs are good bird food.

So, if you find that your birds crave even more shell than they get with their ration of hard-boiled eggs, save the shells from home cooking, but remember to boil or bake them for a half-hour before feeding.

One aspect of nutrition well known but frequently overlooked by beginners in aviculture is that calcium in bones and egg shells requires vitamin D in order to be properly utilized. That is why milk, a high calcium food, is often "fortified" with vitamin D. This vitamin D then with calcium is the anti-rachitic or preventive for rickets, the disease of soft bones.

The natural chemical substance vitamin D is often called the "sunlight vitamin" because it is so closely tied in with solar rays. In fact, the process for making the vitamin D in milk hinges on irradiation (exposure) by certain wave lengths of ultra-violet light naturally emitted by the sun or artificially created by special electrical discharge lamps. The point is simply that direct unfiltered sunlight seems to help birds produce their own vitamin D. So, you should, if possible, give your birds the advantage of a screened aviary, part of which is exposed to direct sunlight a few hours daily. A more sophisticated technique would be to provide ultra-violet light from a lamp. This is difficult, expensive and could be dangerous if overdone. The third method is to provide foods and food supplements which are known to be rich in the various complex fractions of this important substance. You may, if you wish, supplement their diet by adding irradiated cod liver oil to some of the grain you feed, or you might use a vitamin D concentrate available from your pet dealer or pharmacist. As you can see, there are several routes to follow; choose the one that best suits your birds and don't neglect it.

As an aside of considerable interest to people who avoid eating foods containing cholesterol, it should be pointed out that as long ago as 1924, studies of cholesterol and vitamin D showed that ". . .cholesterol, which accompanies most animal fats, and the analogous constituents of vegetable oils, became active antirachitically when they were exposed to ultra-violet radiation." All of this foregoing quotation is from the fourteenth edition of the *Encyclopaedia Britannica*. Actually it is not the cholesterol itself that is activated but a minor component associated with it and known as ergosterol.

Don't worry about cholesterol in your birds' diet causing heart disease. It is very likely that by the time you read this book there will be ample evidence to prove that the quantity of cholesterol that plugs your circulatory system or that of your pet bird has little or nothing to do with the quantity of cholesterol in the diet. Certain animals and people can and do manufacture cholesterol regardless of what they eat.

The other vitamins necessary for the health and fertility of your birds (A, B, C and E) will come naturally if you show intelligent care in providing fresh raw green vegetables, a variety of living seeds (test them occasionally to be sure they sprout) and diet supplements such as fruit, hard boiled or scrambled eggs and wheat germ.

GRIT

Zebra finches, and in fact all seed eaters, swallow whole grains. Small birds husk the seeds but larger species like pigeons, poultry and waterfowl swallow it whole. There is no chewing in the mouth; this is accomplished later in a powerfully muscular organ, the gizzard. Here the seeds and an assortment of grains of sand are squeezed and churned and ground until the seeds break up into a mass of damp flour.

The bird chooses what it needs. You need only provide the grit. Your pet shop, bird store or nearby beach will furnish a supply. Keep it before the birds at all times.

You may also discover that zebras eat charcoal. Good! But the one is no substitute for the other.

VITAMINS

Let's go down the list of vitamins and related substances but don't let it frighten you. A balanced and diversified diet will probably provide all the vitamins your birds will ever need and a vitamin supplement from your pet dealer will guarantee to provide these substances. Here then for the record are their names, natural sources and the diseases of birds which develop when these vitamins are absent.

A—Found in eggs and green vegetables, it improves night vision and resistance to infection, especially of skin. It is possible that excessive dosing of vitamin A causes French molt in budgies.

B—This is the famous anti-beriberi vitamin. Actually it is a "complex" of a dozen or so vitamins. Niacin, for example, is vital for growth and good plumage. Biotin improves egg hatchability.

C—This is the scurvy-preventive citrus fruit vitamin. Also called ascorbic acid. Seed-eating birds seem to manufacture it and so do not require any in their diet.

D—Calcium metabolism depends on vitamin D and the source of it is ultra-violet radiation on some oils and fats. Birds in direct sunlight make their own vitamin D.

E—Found in seed germ , it is destroyed through oxidation by excessive dosage of cod liver oil.

K—Required for coagulation of blood. Produced in the intestines by bacteria and so not required in the diet. Vitamin K is especially vulnerable to antibiotics.

Vitamins A, D, E and K are fat soluble and are often associated with edible oils or fats. Vitamins B and C are water soluble. It is entirely possible that indiscriminate dosing of cagebirds with antibiotics can actually destroy vitamins or at least reduce the ability of the bird to assimilate those vitamins it does ingest.

WATER AND BATHING

Zebra finches are not web-footed but they certainly love to have bathing water close by at all times. A tray or glass dish one inch deep

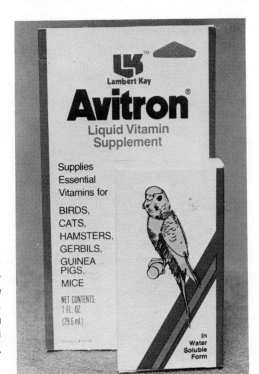

A variety of dietary supplements for birds are available at pet shops. All of them perform specific nutritional functions.

and as large as possible is what they crave. The water depth should be about one-half inch. If the sides of the tray are but one-half inch deep, the loss due to splashing will make a mess. If the tray is much deeper than one inch, the birds will be inhibited, probably because the bath tub will seem too much like a trap. The birds want to jump in and then fly out easily.

Don't get the idea that because you furnish a drinking water dish and a bath water dish that they will use these facilities as you have planned. There will always be a bath water drinker and a drinking water bather. Don't fight it. Just try to keep all the water in the cage or aviary clean and fresh.

That dish of bath water will teach you a lot about your birds. Watch it. Remember that they are inveterate bathers. If each adult zebra finch does not take a dip or two every day, look closely at the water. It is probably not clean enough for *you* to want to drink it. Rinse the dish and fill it with fresh, clean, cool water and most likely all those birds will be in it up to their rumps within minutes. This business of frequent bathing is true for society finches as well, but somewhat less so for many other cagebirds.

If your birds are provided with a bath and the water is fresh and clean and still they don't use it, look to its depth. These little fellows are pretty fussy about how far they wade in before the splashing. The simplest procedure is for you to provide a long bathtub and raise one end an inch and fill the tub until the high end is barely wet. Then, somewhere over that sloped bottom, the water depth will be precisely what the birds prefer. Try it, they'll like it.

Chlorine is frequently added to municipal water supplies to reduce odors and also to reduce the possibility of transmission of diseases. Some birds tolerate small amounts and others seem to resent it. Fortunately chlorine escapes into the air if water is left standing with a large surface exposed. Agitation helps. Boiling helps but is really unnecessary. If your tap water is heavily chlorinated, simply draw off what you need into a gallon plastic milk bottle—fill only up to the level where the bottle begins to neck down—say three quarts, and let it stand uncorked for a day or two. Hot tap water will give up chlorine even faster. Let it stand until it cools, then use it.

Water temperature is not an issue with zebra finches. Serve it at room temperature or if cooler, it will soon reach room temperature. Same goes for bath water. Some zebras will bathe and splash twice daily if you leave water out for them. This is where anodized aluminum rustproof cages and trays earn their keep. Generally, the tray or the bottom of the cage gets most of the punishment from grit, bird droppings and water.

As mentioned elsewhere, but for added emphasis it is worth repeating here, your zebra finches will drink frequently and bathe frequently. They will bathe in their drinking water and drink from their bathing dishes. You may try to force them to do it your way. You probably will not succeed. Why bother? The water should be fresh and clean at all times.

Zebra finches can tolerate intermittent freezing temperatures, but water and some water containers cannot. Your birds will not freeze, but if there is nothing but ice available, they may die of thirst.

It is worth repeating that zebras crave a bath now and then. How frequently? Twice daily if the ice is thin enough to break through. To watch them rattle their wings and tails in a shallow dish of water is to watch birds in bliss. It is obvious to anyone who witnesses these ablutions that these birds are not acting out of duty or boredom or instinct but because they seem to take pleasure in splashing. When one jumps in, the others will follow and for about five minutes pandemonium prevails.

The birds will wet themselves to a point just short of where flying becomes difficult, and then they will flit off to a perch, preferably in bright sunlight for drying, fluffing and preening. The bathing accomplishes several things. It probably helps control lice. It carries off dirt and dead particles of skin and feathers. It moistens the feathers of birds which are incubating eggs and this moisture aids in the hatching process. When eggs with live embryos don't hatch, the fault is frequently with the moisture. Bear in mind that nests in cages don't get the benefit of rain or even the morning dew.

You may substitute a spray in a planted aviary or an outside flight for the bath dish or better still, offer both. For a species without webbed feet, it is really surprising how much zebras demonstrate their enjoyment of the bath.

If you house your birds in an outdoor aviary, you may discover that they capture ants and rub themselves with them or that they stand over an anthill and permit the ants to crawl over themselves. The ants are of the non-stinging varieties and the birds known to do this include 200 species in 30 of the 74 passerine families. Whether zebras also indulge is for you to find out. At this moment, positive evidence is lacking.

If your birds do it, at least we think we know *why*. It seems that formic acid and other similar chemicals generated by many species of ants will keep lice away. Other liquids produced by ants may aid in feather maintenance. Among the Estrildidae, waxbills are known to "ant" and we know that some waxbills have hybridized with zebra finches, so you can go on from there.

These are healthy white zebra finches. Don't buy a bird with a "runny nose" or partly closed eyes—you will be buying trouble.

Dust bathing is another activity your birds may indulge in if you provide the ingredients. Bone dry fine sand or earth is worked into the plumage and then it is shaken out, perhaps for feather maintenance or perhaps for louse control. Some species bathe first in dust and then in water when the situation permits. The common house sparrow, *Passer domesticus domesticus,* is a good example.

Sunbathing is another form of bathing zebra finches will indulge in whenever the opportunity affords. Really, they are very busy "doing things" all the daylight hours, but they are opportunists and when the sun shines, they will spread their feathers and soak in some sun rays. If the sunlight gets to your birds through a glass window it will have lost that vitally important ingredient, ultra-violet, which is the form of radiant energy that triggers the creation of vitamin D. Every bird needs vitamin D for the assimilation of calcium and it may be derived from either direct exposure to sunlight (thus the bird manufactures the vitamin) or by supplements to the food. Your caging arrangements will determine which route to take. Or, take both.

Oiling is still another form of bathing for feather maintenance. Every finch has an oil gland at the base of its tail which it can reach with its bill. The gland is stimulated by rubbing to secrete oil and with its bill, the bird distributes the oil over its feathers. This tends to waterproof them, but the *exact* reason why they do it is not positively known. Some families of birds don't have oil glands, but somehow they do very nicely, even when it rains. There is also reason to believe that oiling has an insulating effect.

Left: This is a typical finch nest basket, popular with bird fanciers and with the birds as well. **Below:** Given a box larger than necessary, zebras will likely produce this result.

Housing

Birds tend to fly horizontally; that is, they travel more horizontal distance than vertical distance in the course of a lifetime. So, you should provide a cage where the greatest distance is horizontal. If you have space and money for three cubic feet of cage, it would be better three feet long by a foot high and a foot wide than three feet high and a foot square on the base. This cage would be large enough for one pair to breed or for four birds to live together wholesomely. If you can provide a larger home for your pets, so much the better. Flying is good for them and maintenance is easier in larger quarters.

If you have direct sunlight available, this is great. Just remember not to let the sun cook your pets. They should always have some place in the cage or aviary where they can roost in the shade and they should also have cool, fresh bath water before them all the time or at least whenever they are exposed to the sun.

1

2

3

(1) A zebra hen broods her newly hatched chicks. (2) This is what happens if you don't provide plenty of extra nests. This basket is overloaded with grass and the eggs of several hens. (3) Here a pair of penguin breeders sit atop their overstuffed next box. Zebras are great for overstuffing their nests.

Buy a cage which is made of anodized aluminum or stainless steel, or chromium plated if you can afford it. In the long run these cages, available in most pet shops, will be the least expensive. Galvanized steel mesh is also durable but not as attractive in the home. A canary cage or a parakeet cage will house a zebra finch as well, but if you have a choice, choose the cage designed for this bird—eventually you may wish to breed zebras and then a large long cage will make a fine breeding establishment.

If you plan on an outdoor ground-level aviary, wonderful! Finches do well in them, especially if they are planted with tough plants. A tender leaf will end up on the floor. Try fruit trees, forsythia and privets. Be sure you have buried galvanized wire mesh deeply (at least a foot) so as to keep out rats, weasels, cats, vermin and other predators.

The ideal screening is three-eighths-inch square mesh (or three eighths by one inch). Most adult zebras will not get through one-half by one-inch mesh (or one-half by one-half). Three-eighths square seems to keep all birds in and all mammals out.

Incidentally, mice are not predators. They don't bite the birds, but nevertheless they can cause the birds to die. Mice are nocturnal and zebras are diurnal, so the zebras (which are caged and unable to get away) will be kept awake until they waste away from lack of sleep. Mice also foul the grain. Call them vermin.

The cage or aviary should have provisions for food, drinking water, bathing water, grit, perching, nesting (if this is what you have in mind) and a place to hang a cuttlebone. Not too difficult or costly when you consider the pleasure these birds will provide.

At night your birds will enjoy roosting in a nest box even if they are not breeding. If you have room in their cage, give them a coconut or a coffee can or a wicker basket. During the day, they will perch on twigs or dowels but you should not force them to use perches with sandpaper. Keep it as natural as you can.

If you place potted plants in your large cage or aviary, the birds certainly will spend a lot of time perching, picking, and climbing. You should aim at something tough and not poisonous. A fruit tree or a privet or a forsythia or a honeysuckle bush might be good to try. If there is not room for a tree, settle for a twig. Red and white cedars are evergreen but a bit coarse. One four-foot cedar tree in the author's aviary boasted never fewer than two well built and productive nests. Don't spend a lot of money on the tree and don't waste your effort on something which is in flower—you may discover that your zebras prefer to have the petals and leaves on the floor, and they will surely accomplish their version of interior decoration in spite of your best laid plans.

By comparison with society finches, you may find that your zebras are somewhat better off in aviaries whereas societies do better in 30 or 36 inch cages—with respect to production.

Cages can be designed for economy of cleaning and feeding effort or for economy of construction or for economy of space. Obviously if you slice the pie thinly enough you would do better with a stuffed bird or a carving or a really good photograph.

On the other hand, caging can become an architectural or decorative part of your home. A large cage can be created to serve as a room divider. Remember as you plan such a project that you will need to remove birds, feed and water them, furnish bath facilities and perching accommodations. You might opt for potted plants as perches and again you should make the doors large enough to get those plants in and out.

Partitions or restraints for the birds are traditionally made of wire mesh or rods but raffia also provides security and in certain decorative schemes it should prove especially attractive. Glass is easy to look through but of course it doesn't permit circulation of air and it also mutes any sounds. If either or both of the walls are close together—say, no more than eighteen inches apart—the risk of injury to a bird by flying into a transparent window is not great. For one thing, your birds will quickly learn to do most of their flying the "long" way and also it would be hard even for a finch to pick up much speed in those narrow confines. Fortunately too zebra finches are not highstrung.

Some zoos have mastered the technique of "caging" birds by means of "walls" of fast-moving currents of air. This may seem a bit sophisticated for even a modern home, but we do have central vacuum systems in many houses today and of course central air conditioning fans operate around the clock.

PESTS

Pests include wild birds, mice, rats, cats and small boys. A young mouse, for instance, can sometimes squeeze through half-inch square screening and by scurrying around at night, rob your birds of sleep and even cause them to hurt themselves as they fly blindly into objects at night. Your birds will not successfully produce clutches of maximum numbers if they are harassed at night by mice or other creatures. You must assure them of a quiet night, every night.

Make up your mind before you invest too much cash or time—do you want to maintain a collection of healthy birds or do you wish to show them off to all comers—smokers, coughers, sneezers, cage rattlers, shouters and arm wavers included?

3

(1,2) Zebras seem to like to do things
such as feeding together, whether it's a
leaf of romaine lettuce or their seed mix.
(3) The quality of this zebra's diet shows
in his perfect condition.

Escapes are easy for all finches, especially zebras. They are inquiring, probing, searching, all day long. If an opening one inch in diameter exists anywhere, they will find it and be out even if they don't really want to go anywhere in particular. If you build an aviary, make the doors as low as you can conveniently bend under. Many escapes take place over your head when a high door is opened. Corridors and arrangements of double doors are ideal for prevention of escapes. The trouble is that you have to open and close twice as many doors in order to make a visit.

When frightened, your aviary birds will fly toward the light, and if the light happens to be coming through a glass window, broken necks and fractured skulls could result. Usually prevention is easy to accomplish. Stretch a cheese-cloth-like fabric over the inside of the window and fasten it to the frame with thumbtacks or staples. Most of the light will still get in but collisions will be cushioned.

Another alternative is to "paint" the window glass inside with a powder-type cleanser such as Bon Ami or calcimine whitewash. These materials even if applied thinly will suffice to warn the birds. Of course, the cheese-cloth offers real protection; the painting is merely a warning.

VISITORS

You should be seen by your zebras. Visit them daily—during the light hours. If you breed a few, handle the babies once their eyes are open, if only to get bands on them. These birds have been with humans for a long time and they seem, instinctively, to get along well with us. They will not become as intimate with you as a budgie or a parrot, but as you care for your birds, you will notice that you are trusted. We all know (and birds know instinctively) that they are vulnerable when they bathe. It is not easy to take off from a muddy wet surface and it is not possible to fly at top speed with wet feathers. Nevertheless, your birds will bathe while you watch them. Under similar circumstances a cordon bleu or an orange-cheeked waxbill would be less likely to bathe with someone hovering nearby.

Cagebirds do well with routine. So, create a routine and then try to live with it. Cage cleaning, feeding, nest inspection and casual visits should all be during the bright light hours, regardless of whether the light is daylight or artificial. Don't let daylight dim and then suddenly turn on brilliant electric lights and expect your birds to appreciate your company. Most zebras will probably tolerate the shock, but rare or delicate species could easily keel over after a few such experiences.

Noise is also a problem you will have to cope with. Again, your birds will adjust to conditions which build up gradually and then repeat themselves at predictable intervals. Look at birds and bats in a belfry. Every hour on the hour a two-ton bronze bell is struck by a hundred pound cast iron hammer and all day long the bats sleep through it and all night long the birds sleep through it. And on Sunday morning at ten or eleven o'clock the call to worship is deafening; yet these animals come back day after day, for generations. *Routine* disturbances are really not disturbances.

If you breed your birds (and this is not especially difficult) decide early on that you will look in the nest once daily, or that you will stay strictly away for the entire six weeks from first egg to flying fledgling. These precautionary notes will be no great imposition on you—but if you are aiming to take that step from owning a cage of birds to becoming a bird keeper, this is how to begin. Here is where we separate the men from the boys, the sheep from the goats, the bird owners from the bird keepers.

CAPTURES

First, to avoid any possible misunderstanding, do not trap or even possess any wild trapped native finches in the U.S.A. It is against federal law to own or traffic in native wild birds. A Philadelphia lawyer might find a few loopholes, but a Philadelphia judge might find the lawyer was wrong. So, to keep out of jail, just don't catch or possess native birds. On the statute books you might be judged a felon.

If your pet escapes you should write it off. The chances of recovery don't justify chasing it down. If your problem is simply inside your aviary or large cage, the first approach should be at night. With patience you may be able to pick up in your hand the bird you want—without a net.

If you must net a bird, buy a net from a dealer who specializes in them. The fabric should be closely woven to avoid entanglements—a ¼-inch mesh or as fine as 1/16-inch would be a good approximation. The size and shape of the hoop will depend on your aviary. One foot square or one foot in diameter is about as small as most people can use effectively. The larger the hoop, the easier the catch, but as the hoop gets larger, it gets unwieldy and perches get in the way.

The hoop might well be wrapped with a soft fabric so that if your bird collides with or is caught under the hoop, it will not suffer broken bones.

If you have your "druthers," you would be well advised to make your captures at night, by hand.

FINCHES AT NIGHT

Your zebra finches are diurnal. They sleep at night and are active dur-

3

(1) A pair of silvers. (2) Fawn male (upper
bird) and silver female. (3) Gray female
(lowest bird), pied fawn female (center
bird), gray male.

There are many different types and sizes of cages available at pet shops. Whichever you choose for your birds, make sure the cage is roomy and the bars not so widely spaced that the birds may escape.

ing the light hours. Actually they will begin to roost for the night about an hour before dusk. The young are fed intermittently during the day only, and it is your job to give them the peace and quiet they are accustomed to at night.

This is especially important for breeders because if a setting adult is kicked off the eggs at night and it is really dark, it may not find its way back and the eggs or fledglings will take a chill—perhaps fatally.

So plan your day around the natural habits of the birds and get the chores done completely at least one hour before dusk. A dim light in or close to the aviary at night may be of value if the birds are scary. A ten watt lamp in a hundred-square-foot room is more than ample and seven and one-half watts will probably suffice. Ten watts for one hundred hours is one kilowatt hour—and that costs less than ten cents. If you have your birds in a large cage or aviary, the lamp might well be mounted under a large "pie pan" reflector and it will then also provide warmth for sick or weak birds. Watch it at night—it may help you spot a health problem.

QUARANTINING NEW BIRDS

If you are interested in adding birds from another aviary, do it only if you are absolutely sure of the health conditions at the source. If in doubt, isolate the newcomers for at least two weeks, preferably in another building, at least in another room. Don't be the carrier of disease as you go from newly introduced birds to your own valued stock.

(1) Chestnut-flanked white pair; a pair of fawns. (2) Maintaining purity of ground color and strength of markings is a problem with the chestnut-flank mutation.

2 —→

Left: The good health of your finches depends a great deal on your ability to feed and house them properly—this chick is enjoying egg food. **Below:** If your zebras have the healthy look of these, you can skip this chapter.

Illness

Start with healthy birds from a reliable source. Keep them dry and out of drafts. Feed them good millet and supplement the millet with other grains, green vegetables, minerals, grit, clean water. Don't introduce sick birds or even birds which haven't been in a quarantine of some sort. Let them sleep all night every night without interruption, no noisy mice, no flashing lights. Give them sufficient room.

All right, you did all that. Now enjoy your birds; chances are good they will never have a sick day. But what if they do, you with the hardy zebras ask.

First, go over the checklist of food, water, shelter—the basics. Then evaluate the damage. Did you simply lose one bird because it flew into a window and broke its neck or is there an epidemic in your aviary? Look for signs. Ruffled feathers, eyes that appear small, much daytime sleeping, little eating, wet vents, running nostrils, no chirping.

(1, 2) Silver male, with inset showing cheek-patch variation. (3, 4) Cream male.

1

2

(1, 2) Silver female. (3, 4) Cream female.

3

4

You will have to be a detective because most bird diseases are hard to diagnose positively without an autopsy.

There are several courses of action after you have gone over the obvious things first. See a veterinarian and be prepared to pay for the visit. He may have to work as hard on your bird as he does on Fifi, the three hundred dollar poodle.

Second, study the diseases of birds in a specialized book. There are several. Stroud's book on canary diseases is applicable to zebra finches as well. Another excellent textbook is *Bird Diseases* by Arnall and Keymer. This is a 528 page classic, profusely illustrated in color.

Third, apply several general therapies which have saved many birds in the past. Work fast. Bird diseases frequently gallop. Raise the temperature to 85-90 °F. and hold it until there is recovery. Then lower it *gradually* over several days to the normal cage or aviary temperature. Add a broad base antibiotic such as Aureomycin or tetracycline to the drinking water. These drugs are great to cure disease, but if you use them constantly they will destroy all the normal bacteria in the bird's digestive system; the bird will be cured of disease but will starve to death even if fed heavily because, without the bacteria, no bird will digest its food.

Offer food treats, keep the cage clean, don't interrupt sleep, remove infected birds or otherwise segregate healthy birds from unhealthy ones, if possible. The Arnall and Keymer book previously mentioned is very comprehensive and detailed, so you have a real task if the general remedies don't work.

PARASITES

Birds are also bothered by other cage companions you should eliminate. These are the many species of jointed-leg creatures. Here we consider the animals in the tremendous phylum Arthropoda including the class Insecta and the class Arachnida. The insects include mosquitoes, flies and lice. The arachnids include mites, ticks and spiders.

In both classes some are scavengers and some are parasites. "Some" is the wrong word—there are hundreds of species, some known, some unknown, some large enough to swat, others so small you need a microscope merely to see them and a high-power microscope to examine them. Don't bother; it will get you nowhere.

Bird lice are a bother which you will control, but many species of mites and all ticks are genuine enemies which you must actively fight. Fortunately the life style of the parasitic mite helps you win the battle

This pair of zebras have been segregated in a breeding cage. This is the only way you can be sure of the parentage of the off-spring.

against it. It is a nocturnal feeder. During the night, the mite sucks blood and during the day it hides and deposits eggs—in crevices and cracks of the cage or aviary.

So, during the daylight hours your birds are rid of the mites and you should take advantage of this fact. Place a white cotton rag over a cage of birds in the evening before you retire. Examine it the following morning after your breakfast. Mites will have crawled off the birds and settled in the folds of the cloth. Good. Fold up the cloth and burn it. Then, that same morning put your mite-infested birds into a cage which you recently sterilized with washing soda and boiling water and then you should sterilize the cage they had been in. Get into all the hiding places in the aviary with gamma benzene hexachloride. Do this once every ten days for three or four cycles, and you will have wiped out most or all the mites. Then do it once every other month or sooner if the mites show up again.

Ticks need the mechanical picking or chemical treatments mentioned below and lice, mosquitoes, flies will succumb to pyrethrum compounds, paradichlorobenzene or a no-pest strip used intermittently. Remember that a light spray or dusting of pyrethrum is safe for all birds including finches, but too much exposure to a no-pest strip or to gamma benzene hexachloride might possibly be dangerous for some of the more delicate species of birds. If convenient, move the birds out while any high-power insecticide is working.

1

2

(1, 2) Two views of a crested gray male. (3, 4) A crested fawn penguin female. (5) A young crested gray female. (6, 7) Back and front views of the rare black-breast mutation.

5

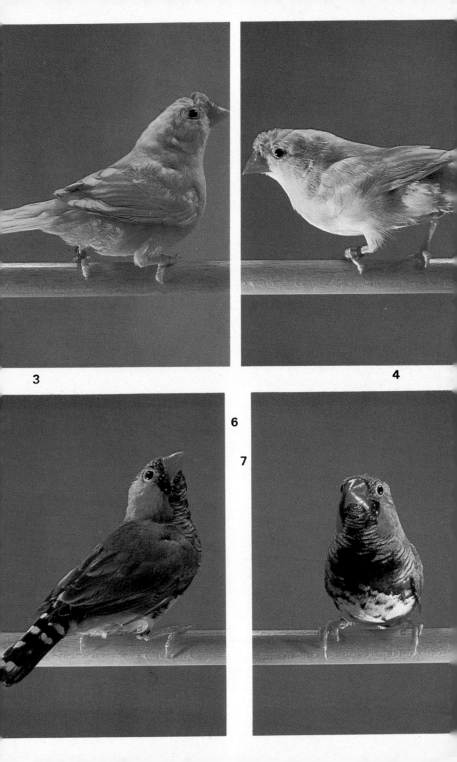

3

4

6

7

Paradichlorobenzene, the famous clothes-moth control, is effective against lice and mice. Put some crystals near a louse-infested cage for a few days now and then, and if the treatment proves effective, continue it.

Some bird keepers report that they control some arthropod pests with a spray they mix. It contains one part of Listerine and four parts of Witch Hazel, but there is not now and probably never will be one certain cut-and-dried sure control for these pests and parasites.

Don't waste your time trying to identify lice, fleas, ticks and mites. One reliable source of information about them states that of the million known species of arthropods, there are more than twenty-five hundred species of lice which are associated with birds. Additionally, there are fifteen hundred species of fleas, many of which parasitize birds. There are more than fifteen thousand species of ticks and mites, of which there are hundreds found only on birds. Frequently the host-parasite relationships are complicated. One bird may have several lice, flea and mite species on or in its skin, feathers, nasal passages or leg scales. Some of these arthropods eat other arthropods and some limit their activity to feces or wastes which accumulate in the nest. A cage or aviary bird wholly rid of all these pests would be unusual, to say the least. Of course you should aim to eliminate them, but nevertheless be satisfied even if you merely succeed in controlling them.

Several government agencies concerned with our personal or environmental health have established rules and guidelines for manufacturers of insect control chemicals. These rules lead to tests which should assure than an insecticide is not dangerous to any but a particular organism. Unfortunately, these tests are time-consuming and expensive. Many proven lice, mite and tick remedies of the past are no longer in the marketplace. Worse, there are not apt to be any substitutes for them in the foreseeable future because the cost of proving their safety would wipe out any possible profit. The old books (and this one does too) mention preparations which may be banned by the time you read these words. Join a fanciers' association, subscribe to a magazine, talk to your pet shop proprietor. These are the only ways you will be able to keep current with the insecticide business.

BONES

Once in a great while a caged finch will break a leg or a wing. Many bird keepers have kept hundreds of finches for decades and never had it happen, but it might.

If this is as a result of frail bones because of a calcium deficiency, you should look to minerals and vitamin D. If the problem is in the cage design, the answer will be obvious. To the extent that long toenails may prevent a bird from properly perching on its perch, resulting in a fall which could cause a broken wing or leg, then the toenails need a clipping.

What to do with the injured bird? You decide, but here are a few hints and guidelines. Splints consisting of a ¼ inch by 3/8 inch piece of transparent household mending tape have been used with success by some fanciers. A hospital cage with no perches, quiet isolation, warmth and rest sometimes suffice for spontaneous mending of the broken bone. Amputation is sometimes necessary. One-legged birds will thrive for their normal lifespan, but they will not breed since both legs are needed for a bird to keep its balance during copulation.

Wings are even less frequently broken and they generally mend within three weeks of quiet isolation in a hospital cage. There is not much you can do about a broken wing on a finch, but if you wish to go to the expense, you might consult your veterinarian.

CLAWS

The normal length of the four claws ("nails") on each foot is perhaps 1/16 or 1/8 inch longer than the part with a blood supply in it. If the nails grow corkscrewed or overly long, perching and even hopping will become difficult. Should such a long-nailed bird attempt to incubate a clutch of eggs, it will surely puncture a few.

Clip the nails of finches with a fingernail clipper or small sharp scissors. You will be able to see the blood vessels when you look through the nails toward the light. Clip 1/16 inch beyond the end of this pink portion. If you inadvertently draw blood, and really this is unnecessary, touch the claw end with a styptic pencil or a little alum powder and the slight bleeding will immediately stop.

Many birds go through their years of life with no nail clipping, so don't do it routinely, but rather on an infrequent as-needed basis.

FEATHER PLUCKING

You will not confuse natural normal molting with feather plucking. The molt is usually a seasonal summertime thing. The molting bird does not end up with bald spots; it just looks a bit ragged for several weeks.

Feather plucking is a vice. Some birds do it to other birds. Isolate the offender and the victim or victims will recover in a month or two. Some birds do it to themselves. Frequently the cause is overcrowding or lack of minerals, especially salt in the diet. These are things you can correct. Sometimes mites are the irritant and the bird tears out its own

(1) A fawn male. (2) A juvenile black-breasted male. (3, 4) Black-breasted male; note lack of barring on uppertail coverts in this bird.

(1, 2) A white male; note flecking on back, a show fault that sometimes disappears in subsequent molts. (3, 4) A black-breasted female.

feathers as it scratches sore spots. Your pet supply store probably handles anti-plucking sprays which may be applied to the victim. These are frequently effective but you would be well advised to search out the cause and correct it, rather than to go only after the symptom. If you have a pair with an aggressive male and an uncooperative female, you may be witnessing some pre-nuptial funny business. This generally shows up as a loss of feathers on the back of the neck of the female. She will probably recover completely and go on to raise a big healthy family.

SOFT MOLT

If you are inconsistent about the cage lighting and do not establish a pattern for hours of light and hours of darkness, the metabolic processes of your birds will be affected adversely. In plain simple language they will molt out of season. This condition is termed "soft molt" and the bird in soft molt never looks quite right. Its feathers will always be ragged and its overall appearance will look wrong to you. Even if you can't put your finger on the problem precisely, you will just know something is not quite right. When this happens to you, you are metamorphosing from being a bird owner to being a bird keeper. But that doesn't help your bird. What the bird needs is a carefully controlled astronomical clock to turn the lights on early every day or turn them off late every night so that the cage is illuminated at *regular* intervals of about 13 hours on and 11 hours off.

If this supplement to daylight is on a simple on-off clock switch, it should be accompanied by a dim night light so the birds are never stranded in total darkness when that clock turns the bright light off.

DISEASE AND WATER

The few diseases and parasites your birds may have or may get are often transmitted from one bird to another when fecal matter gets into the food or drinking water. This is something you must (and can easily) control. Don't arrange the cage or aviary so that a perch is located over food or water. Do change water dishes frequently and wash them thoroughly before you refill them.

For caged birds you might provide bathing water separate from drinking water and remove the bath tub promptly after it has been used. One half inch or so is ample depth for the bath water.

Drinking water is often the vehicle for antibiotic medicines and also for vitamin food supplements. The only problem you may encounter is that some birds would rather get thirsty than drink water which has been tampered with. This then is a place where you will have to use some of your own intelligence as you proceed.

Don't expect baby finches to bathe until they are fully fledged—three months would be about the youngest age at which they might voluntarily go into water, and a month or less will not make any difference to the health of your bird.

THE HOSPITAL CAGE

Your birds are naturally vigorous and disease resistant. It is entirely reasonable to expect that a well-cared for finch could live out its entire eight to twelve years in a cage or an aviary with no medical care. The only time you might touch it would be to clip its nails.

If you should acquire an ill bird or if an accident should befall a pet finch, your first corrective step should be by way of *isolation* and *warmth*. Buy or build a hospital cage. It need not be very large. A fifteen inch cube would suffice. It should have a low perch, water, food supply and *controlled warmth*. Controlled warmth is a big item in the cure of most cage bird ailments, and for these little fellows 85 or 90° F is what they need.

A heater should be coupled with an adjustable thermostat and the ideal arrangements for this have long been worked out and are available through pet dealers or cage bird magazine advertisements. If you feel you cannot afford the manufactured product, look at one and pirate the design. The best source of heat is electricity—25 watts will probably suffice; 50 would be more than ample. The adjustable feature of the thermostat is important because after the bird recovers from its ailment, the temperature should be lowered gradually to that of the normal room over the course of several additional days before ending the treatment. For egg binding, colds, constipation and general malaise, you begin with warmth and then treat the specific symptom if you are able to recognize it.